TREATS

just great recipes

GENERAL INFORMATION

The level of difficulty of the recipes in this book
is expressed as a number from 1 (simple) to 3 (difficult).

TREATS
just great recipes

gelato

McRae Books

SERVES 4–6
PREPARATION 20 min + 30 min to chill
and time to churn
COOKING 15 min
DIFFICULTY level 1

Basic Gelato

Place a large bowl in the freezer to chill. • Place the milk, cream, lemon zest, and half the sugar in a heavy-based saucepan over medium-low heat and bring to a boil. • Remove from the heat and discard the lemon zest. • Beat the egg yolks and remaining sugar in a medium bowl with an electric mixer on high speed until pale and creamy. • Pour the hot milk mixture over the egg mixture, beating constantly with a wooden spoon. Return the mixture to the saucepan. Simmer over very low heat, stirring constantly, until it just coats the back of the spoon. Do not let the mixture boil. • Remove from the heat and pour into the chilled bowl. Let cool completely, stirring often. • Chill in the refrigerator for 30 minutes. • Transfer the mixture to your ice cream machine and freeze following the manufacturer's instructions. • Alternatively, if you don't have an ice cream machine, place the mixture in a metal bowl and freeze. When it has just begun to set, whisk it with an electric beater or by hand until creamy. Repeat at least 3 or 4 more times or until thick, smooth, and scoopable.

2 cups (500 ml) milk
2 cups (500 ml) heavy (double) cream
Zest of 1/2 a lemon, removed using a sharp knife
1 1/2 cups (300 g) sugar
8 large egg yolks

Vanilla Gelato

Place a large bowl in the freezer to chill. • Place 3½ cups (875 ml) of milk in a heavy-based saucepan with the coffee beans, cinnamon stick, lemon zest, vanilla pod, and salt over medium-low heat. Mix well and bring to a boil. Lower the heat and simmer gently for 10 minutes. • Beat the egg yolks, sugar, and cornstarch in a medium bowl with an electric mixer on high speed until pale and creamy. • With mixer on low speed, add the remaining cold milk followed by the hot milk mixture. Return to the saucepan and simmer over very low heat, stirring constantly, for 2 minutes. Do not let the mixture boil. • Remove from the heat and filter into the chilled bowl. Let cool completely, stirring often. • Chill in the refrigerator for 30 minutes. • Beat the egg whites until stiff peaks form and fold them into the mixture just before you transfer it to your ice cream machine. Freeze following the manufacturer's instructions.

4 cups (1 liter) milk
6 coffee beans
1 small (about 1-inch/2.5-cm long) cinnamon stick
Small piece of lemon zest, removed using a sharp knife
1 large vanilla pod
⅛ teaspoon salt
1 cup (200 g) sugar
5 large egg yolks
½ teaspoon cornstarch (cornflour)
2 large egg whites

Chocolate sauce, to serve (see page 26)
Fresh berry fruit, and hazelnuts, to serve

SERVES 4

PREPARATION 30 min + time to churn

COOKING 15 min

DIFFICULTY level 1

Gelato

flecked with chocolate

Place a large bowl into the freezer to chill. • Place the milk, lemon zest, vanilla pod, and half the sugar in a large saucepan over medium heat. Mix well and bring to a boil. • Remove from the heat as soon as it reaches a boil. Let cool. Discard the lemon zest and vanilla pod. • Beat the eggs and remaining sugar in a large bowl until pale and creamy. • Gradually add the milk mixture, stirring well. • Return to the saucepan and simmer over very low heat, stirring constantly with a wooden spoon, until the mixture coats the back of the spoon, 7–10 minutes. Be careful not to let the custard boil. • Remove from the heat and transfer to the chilled bowl. Let the custard cool completely, stirring from time to time. • Transfer the mixture to an ice cream machine and freeze following the manufacturer's instructions. • Whip the cream in a large bowl until stiff. When the ice cream is half frozen, add the cream and chocolate.

4 cups (1 liter) milk

Zest of ½ a lemon, removed using a sharp knife

½ vanilla pod

¾ cup (150 g) sugar

5 large eggs

⅓ cup (90 ml) heavy (double) cream

4 oz (125 g) dark chocolate, finely chopped

8

Lemon Sorbet

with peaches and apricots

Place the sugar and water in a saucepan and bring to a boil. Simmer for 3–4 minutes, then set aside to cool. • When the mixture is completely cool stir in the juice of 4 lemons. • Whisk the egg whites and salt until very stiff in a freezerproof bowl. • Gradually stir in the lemon syrup and place in the freezer. Stir every 30 minutes to make sure it freezes evenly. After three hours whisk the mixture, then return to the freezer for another 30 minutes. • Serve in individual dishes with the fruit sprinkled with remaining sugar and lemon juice.

1 cup (200 g) sugar + 2 tablespoons
4½ cups (560 ml) water
Freshly squeezed juice of 5 lemons
3 large egg whites
Pinch of salt
3 large peaches, thinly sliced
3 apricots, thinly sliced

Chocolate Gelato

Place the milk and cream in a medium saucepan over medium heat. Add ¾ cup (150 g) of sugar and the vanilla. Bring to a boil then remove from the heat. • Add the chocolate, stirring until dissolved. • Beat the egg yolks and remaining sugar in a medium bowl with an electric mixer at high speed until pale and creamy. • Beat the cocoa into the egg mixture. • Gradually pour the milk and cream mixture into the egg yolk mixture, stirring well with a wooden spoon. • Return the mixture to the saucepan over low heat and, stirring constantly with a wooden spoon, simmer until it coats the back of the spoon. Make sure the mixture does not boil. • Remove from the heat and strain into a chilled bowl. Let cool. • Place in an ice cream maker and prepare according to the manufacturers' instructions.

2 cups (500 ml) milk
2 cups (500 ml) heavy (double) cream
1¼ cups (250 g) sugar
1 teaspoon vanilla extract (essence)
4 oz (125 g) dark chocolate, coarsely grated
8 large egg yolks
⅓ cup (50 g) unsweetened cocoa powder

SERVES 4–6

PREPARATION 30 min + time to churn

COOKING 15 min

DIFFICULTY level 2

Gelato
with double chocolate

Place the chocolate in a large bowl and set aside. • Beat the egg yolks and sugar with an electric mixer at high speed until pale and creamy. • Bring the cream and milk to a boil in a saucepan over medium heat. • Pour half the hot cream mixture into the egg mixture, beating constantly. Return to the pan with the remaining cream mixture and return to medium heat. Stir constantly until it coats the back of a metal spoon. • Remove from the heat and pour over the chocolate. Stir until the chocolate has melted and the mixture is smooth. Let cool completely. • Stir in the chocolate chips.• Place in an ice cream machine and churn according to the manufacturers' instructions.

8 oz (250 g) dark chocolate, chopped
6 large egg yolks
$\frac{1}{2}$ cup (100 g) superfine (caster) sugar
2 cups (500 ml) heavy (double) cream
1 cup (250 ml) milk
5 oz (150 g) dark chocolate chips

SERVES 4–6

PREPARATION 30 min + time to churn

COOKING 15 min

DIFFICULTY level 2

Mint Gelato
with chocolate chips

Beat the egg yolks and sugar with an electric mixer on high speed until pale and creamy. • Bring the cream and milk to a boil in a saucepan over medium heat. • Remove from the heat. Beat half of the hot cream mixture into the egg mixture. Return to the pan with the milk and cream and return to the heat. Stir continuously until it coats the back of a metal spoon. • Remove from the heat, pour into another bowl, cover, and let cool completely. • Add the chocolate and peppermint extract. • Place in an ice cream machine and churn according to the manufacturers' instructions.

6 large egg yolks
1/2 cup (100 g) superfine (caster) sugar
2 cups (500 ml) light (single) cream
1 cup (250 ml) milk
5 oz (150 g) dark chocolate, chopped
1/4 teaspoon mint extract (essence)

SERVES 4–6
PREPARATION 15 min + 30 min to chill
and time to churn
COOKING 15 min
DIFFICULTY level 2

Coffee Gelato

Place a large bowl in the freezer to chill. • Place the milk and coffee in a heavy-based saucepan over medium heat and bring to a boil. Remove from the heat and stir in the cream and vanilla. • Beat the egg yolks and sugar in a large bowl with an electric mixer on high speed until very pale and creamy. • Pour the hot milk and coffee mixture over the egg mixture, beating constantly with a wooden spoon. Return the mixture to the saucepan. Simmer over very low heat, stirring constantly, until it just coats the back of the spoon. Do not let the mixture boil. • Remove from the heat and pour into the chilled bowl. Let cool completely, stirring often. • Chill in the refrigerator for 30 minutes. • Transfer the mixture to an ice cream machine and freeze following the manufacturer's instructions. • Decorate with the coffee beans and whipped cream just before serving.

2 cups (500 ml) milk
2 tablespoons instant coffee granules
2 cups (500 ml) heavy (double) cream
2 teaspoons vanilla extract (essence)
6 large egg yolks
1¼ cups (250 g) sugar
Coffee beans, to serve
Whipped cream, to serve

SERVES 4
PREPARATION 20 min + 30 min to chill and time to churn
COOKING 15 min
DIFFICULTY level 2

Gelato

with hazelnuts and chocolate

Chop the hazelnuts and confectioners' sugar in a food processor until smooth. • Melt the chocolate in a double boiler over barely simmering water. • Stir the chocolate into the hazelnut mixture and set aside. • Beat the egg yolks and sugar in a medium bowl with an electric mixer on high speed until pale and creamy. • Place the milk and cream in a medium saucepan over medium heat and bring to a boil. • Pour the hot milk mixture over the egg mixture beating constantly with a whisk. • Return to low heat and beat constantly until the mixture coats the back of a metal spoon. Make sure that the mixture does not boil. • Remove from the heat and pour a little of the hot milk mixture into the chocolate mixture. Stir well then pour the chocolate mixture into the hot milk. Beat with a whisk until cool. Chill in the refrigerator for 30 minutes. • Transfer the mixture to an ice cream machine and churn following the manufacturer's instructions.

$1/4$ cup (30 g) toasted (unsalted) hazelnuts + extra, to garnish
2 tablespoons confectioners' (icing) sugar
3 oz (90 g) dark chocolate
4 large egg yolks
$3/4$ cup (150 g) sugar
$2^1/_2$ cups (600 ml) milk
$1/2$ cup (125 ml) heavy (double) cream
Chocolate Sauce, to serve (see page 26)

SERVES 4
PREPARATION 15 min + 30 min to chill and time to churn
COOKING 15 min
DIFFICULTY level 2

Malaga Gelato

Rinse the raisins. Drain well and place in a small bowl. Cover with the Moscato or rum and let plump while you prepare the ice cream. • Place a large bowl in the freezer to chill. • Place the milk and cream in a heavy-based saucepan over medium heat and bring to a boil. • Beat the egg yolks and sugar in a medium bowl with an electric mixer on high speed until pale and creamy. • Pour the hot milk mixture into the bowl with the egg yolk mixture, stirring constantly with a wooden spoon. Return to the saucepan and simmer over very low heat, stirring constantly, until it just coats the back of the spoon. Do not let the mixture boil. • Remove from the heat and transfer to the chilled bowl. Let the mixture cool completely, stirring often. Chill in the refrigerator for 30 minutes. • Transfer the mixture to an ice cream machine and churn following the manufacturer's instructions. Add the raisins and their liquid 1–2 minutes before the gelato is ready.

½ cup (90 g) Malaga or other plump tasty raisins
¼ cup (60 ml) Moscato dessert wine (or rum)
2 cups (500 ml) milk
¾ cup (200 ml) heavy (double) cream
6 large egg yolks
¾ cup (150 g) sugar

21

SERVES 4–6
PREPARATION 30 min + 30 min to chill and time to churn
COOKING 15 min
DIFFICULTY level 2

Squash Gelato
with amaretti cookies

Place a large bowl in the freezer to chill. • Peel the winter squash, remove the seeds, and slice. Steam until just tender, 8–10 minutes. Let cool and then lightly squeeze with your hands to remove as much moisture as possible. • Weigh out 1 pound (500 g) of squash. Place in a food processor with the sugar and salt and chop until smooth. • Place the cream in a heavy-based saucepan over medium heat and bring to a boil. Remove from the heat and stir into the squash mixture. Add the almond extract. • Pour into the chilled bowl. Let cool completely, stirring often. Chill in the refrigerator for 30 minutes. • Transfer the mixture to an ice cream machine and churn following the manufacturer's instructions. • Crumble half the amaretti cookies into serving bowls or glasses. Top with the ice cream and top with the whole amaretti cookies.

4 lb (2 kg) winter squash or pumpkin
¾ cup (150 g) sugar
⅛ teaspoon salt
1⅔ cups (400 ml) heavy (double) cream
2–3 drops almond extract (essence)
About 20 crisp amaretti cookies (biscuits)

Port Gelato

Place a large bowl in the freezer to chill. • Place the milk, cream, orange zest, and half the sugar in a heavy-based saucepan over medium-low heat and bring to a boil. • Remove from the heat and discard the orange zest. • Beat the egg yolks and remaining sugar in a medium bowl with an electric mixer on high speed until pale and creamy. • Pour the hot milk mixture over the egg mixture, beating constantly with a wooden spoon. Return the mixture to the saucepan. Simmer over very low heat, stirring constantly, until it just coats the back of the spoon. Do not let the mixture boil. • Remove from the heat and pour into the chilled bowl. Let cool completely, stirring often. Stir in the port wine. • Chill in the refrigerator for 30 minutes. • Transfer the mixture to an ice cream machine and churn following the manufacturer's instructions. • Serve the gelato garnished with candied cherries and slices of orange and ice cream wafers.

2 cups (500 ml) milk
2 cups (500 ml) heavy (double) cream
Zest of 1/2 an orange removed using a sharp knife
1 1/2 cups (300 g) sugar
8 large egg yolks
1/2 cup (125 ml) dry white port
Candied cherries, to garnish
Thin slices of orange (with peel), to garnish
Ice cream wafers, to serve

SERVES 4–6

PREPARATION 30 min + time to churn

COOKING 15 min

DIFFICULTY level 2

Rice Gelato

with chocolate sauce

Gelato: Place the milk, rice, vanilla pod, and golden raisins in a heavy-based saucepan over medium heat. Bring to a boil then turn the heat down to low. Stir in the salt. Simmer, stirring constantly, until the rice is tender, about 15 minutes. • Remove from the heat and discard the vanilla pod. Let cool completely, stirring from time to time. • Stir in the orange zest, lemon zest, lemon juice, and honey or molasses. • Transfer the mixture to an ice cream machine and freeze following the manufacturer's instructions. • Chocolate Sauce: Place the chocolate and half the milk in a saucepan over medium heat and bring to a boil. • Dissolve the cornflour in the remaining milk and mix into the chocolate along with the sugar. Stir constantly over low heat until thickened. Remove from the heat and whisk until smooth. • When the gelato is ready, spoon it into serving dishes and drizzle with the chocolate sauce. Garnish with the extra raisins and serve.

Gelato
4 cups (1 liter) milk
¾ cup (150 g) pudding rice
1 vanilla pod, sliced open lengthwise
⅓ cup (60 g) golden raisins (sultanas) + extra, to garnish
⅛ teaspoon salt
Finely grated zest of 1 orange
Finely grated zest and juice of 1 lemon
2 tablespoons honey or rice molasses

Chocolate Sauce
8 oz (250 g) dark chocolate, grated
1½ cups (375 ml) cups milk
2 scant teaspoons cornstarch (cornflour)
¼ cup (50 g) superfine (caster) sugar

SERVES 4–6

PREPARATION 15 min + 30 min to chill
and time to churn

COOKING 15 min

DIFFICULTY level 2

Cherry Gelato

Mix the skim milk powder and sugar in a heavy-based saucepan and then add the milk, cream, and salt. • Place over high heat and, just before it begins to boil, turn the heat down to low and simmer for 2 minutes, stirring constantly. • Remove from the heat, add the amarene cherry syrup, and beat with a whisk on medium speed until cool. Chill in the refrigerator for 30 minutes. • Beat with a whisk for 2–3 minutes. Transfer the mixture to an ice cream machine and churn following the manufacturer's instructions. • Cut the amarene cherries in half—leave a few whole to decorate—and add them to the ice cream machine one minute before you turn it off. Decorate with the whole cherries.

1 oz (30 g) skim milk powder
3/4 cup (150 g) sugar
13/4 cups (450 ml) milk
11/3 cups (300 ml) heavy (double) cream
1/8 teaspoon salt
2 tablespoons amarene cherry syrup
4 oz (125 g) canned amarene cherries (drained weight)

SERVES 4–6

PREPARATION 40 min + time to churn

COOKING 15 min

DIFFICULTY level 2

Lemon Gelato

Cut the lemons in half horizontally and scoop out the flesh using a teaspoon. Place in a bowl lined with a piece of muslin. • Arrange the hollowed out lemons on a large tray and place in the freezer. • Wrap the lemon flesh in the muslin and squeeze the juice into the bowl. You should have a generous ¾ cup (200 ml) of lemon juice. • Heat 1¼ cups (250 g) of sugar with the water and salt in a large heavy-based saucepan over low heat. Stir until the sugar has completely dissolved, 3–4 minutes. • Remove from the heat and add the milk and lemon juice. Mix well and let cool. • Beat the egg whites in a large bowl with an electric mixer on high speed until stiff. Add the remaining sugar and beat until stiff and glossy. • Carefully fold into the lemon mixture. Transfer the mixture to an ice cream machine and churn following the manufacturer's instructions. • When the gelato is ready, spoon it into the frozen lemon skins. Store in the freezer until ready to serve. If liked, garnish with grated lemon zest.

8 large lemons, unblemished and of even size
1¾ cups (350 g) sugar
1 cup (250 ml) water
⅛ teaspoon salt
¾ cup (200 ml) milk
2 large egg whites
Finely grated lemon zest, to garnish (optional)

Berryfruit Gelato
with chantilly cream

Purée 1 lb (500 g) of the berries in a blender with ¼ cup (50 g) of the sugar and the water until smooth. • Press the purée through a fine mesh strainer to remove the seeds. • Place the milk, cream, and remaining sugar in a heavy-based saucepan over medium heat. Stir until the sugar has completely dissolved and bring to a boil. • Remove from the heat and let cool completely. • Add the berry fruit purée and mix well. • Transfer to an ice cream machine and churn following the manufacturer's instructions. • Chantilly Cream: Place the cream, confectioners' sugar, and vanilla in a medium bowl and beat with an electric mixer on high speed until thick. • Serve the gelato with the chantilly and remaining berries spooned over each serving.

1½ lb (750 g) fresh mixed berries (raspberries, strawberries, red currants, black currant, blueberries, cloud berries, etc)
1½ cups (300 g) sugar
2 tablespoons water
2 cups (500 ml) milk
1 cup (250 ml) heavy (double) cream

Chantilly Cream
1 cup (250 ml) heavy (double) cream
2 tablespoons confectioners' (icing) sugar
1 teaspoon vanilla extract (essence)

SERVES 4–6

PREPARATION 15 min + time to churn

COOKING 15 min

DIFFICULTY level 2

Coconut Gelato
with raspberry sauce

Place the coconut milk and sugar in a medium bowl and stir until the sugar has dissolved. Stir in the coconut extract and most of the coconut. • Transfer the mixture to an ice cream machine and freeze following the manufacturer's instructions. • Raspberry Sauce: Place the raspberries in a bowl and sprinkle with the confectioners' sugar. Drizzle with the liqueur. Mash well with a fork and set aside. If liked, strain the sauce to remove the seeds (or serve as is). • Place scoops of gelato in serving dishes—or in coconut shells—and drizzle with the sauce. Sprinkle with the remaining coconut.

4 cups (1 liter) unsweetened coconut milk
3/4 cup (150 g) sugar
1/2 teaspoon coconut extract (essence)
1 cup (175 g) unsweetened shredded (desiccated) coconut

Raspberry Sauce
1 lb (500 g) fresh raspberries
3 tablespoons confectioners' (icing) sugar
2 tablespoons raspberry liqueur

SERVES 6–8

PREPARATION 25 min + 2 h to freeze

DIFFICULTY level 1

Gelato Cake
with fresh fruit

You can make this delicious ice cream cake using any two gelato flavors from this book or, if you are short of time, buy two readymade flavors of ice cream of your choice. • Line a 10-inch (25-cm) springform pan with aluminum foil. • Spoon the basic gelato into the prepared pan, followed by the lemon gelato. Cover with aluminum and freeze for 2 hours. • Beat the cream, confectioners' sugar, and vanilla in a large bowl with an electric mixer at high speed until stiff. • Loosen and remove the pan sides. Turn the gelato cake out onto a serving plate. • Decorate with the cream and fresh fruit.

1 quart (liter) Basic Gelato
    (see page 4), softened
1 quart (liter) Lemon Gelato
    (see page 30), softened
2 cups (500 ml) heavy (double) cream
2 tablespoons confectioners' (icing) sugar
1 teaspoon vanilla extract (essence)
15 strawberries, hulled
3 kiwifruit, peeled and thickly sliced

Gelato Cake

with chocolate gelato

Mix the wafer crumbs, butter, and liqueur or syrup in a medium bowl until well blended. • Press into the bottom of a 9-inch (23-cm) springform pan. Refrigerate for 30 minutes. • Beat the gelato in a large bowl with an electric mixer at low speed until creamy. • Spread evenly into the cookie crust. Freeze for 2 hours. • Loosen and remove the pan sides. Place the cake on a serving plate and sprinkle with the chocolate. Let stand at room temperature for 10 minutes.

1½ cups vanilla wafer (plain vanilla biscuit) crumbs

⅓ cup (90 g) butter, melted

1 tablespoon coffee liqueur or chocolate syrup

1 quart (liter) Chocolate Gelato (see page 11), or storebought chocolate ice cream, softened

4 oz (125 g) dark chocolate, coarsely grated

SERVES 6–8

PREPARATION 30 min + 30 min to chill
and time to churn

DIFFICULTY level 1

Gelato Cake
with coffee and chocolate

Gelato: Bring the milk and cream to a boil in a saucepan over medium heat. Remove from the heat. • Beat the egg yolks, sugar, and hot milk mixture in a double boiler until well blended. Cook, stirring constantly with a wooden spoon, until the mixture lightly coats a metal spoon. Add the vanilla. Remove from the heat and stir until cooled. • Chill in the refrigerator for 30 minutes. • Transfer the mixture to an ice cream machine and freeze following the manufacturer's instructions. • Divide the ice cream into two equal portions. Stir the chocolate into one portion and the coffee into the other. • Spoon the mixture into a 10-inch (25-cm) ring mold in layers. Freeze for at least 1 hour. • To Serve: Beat the cream, brandy, and confectioners' sugar in a large bowl with an electric mixer at high speed until stiff. • Unmold the gelato cake onto a serving plate. Pipe the cream over the cake in a decorative manner.

Gelato
2 cups (500 ml) milk
1/2 cup (125 ml) heavy (double) cream
4 large egg yolks
1/2 cup (100 g) sugar
2 teaspoons vanilla extract (essence)
1/4 cup (30 g) confectioners' (icing) sugar
4 oz (125 g) dark chocolate, coarsely chopped
1/2 cup (125 ml) strong black coffee

To Serve
2 cups (500 ml) heavy (double) cream
2 tablespoons brandy
2 tablespoons confectioners' sugar

SERVES 4–6

PREPARATION 45 min + 12 h to freeze

COOKING 5 min

DIFFICULTY level 2

Semifreddo
with vanilla and milk chocolate

Place the chocolate in a bowl. • Bring one-third of the cream to a boil and pour over the chocolate. Stir until the chocolate is melted and smooth. Let cool completely. • Beat the egg yolks and half the sugar with an electric mixer on high speed until pale and creamy. • Beat the egg whites and remaining sugar with mixer on high speed until firm peaks form. • Fold the whites into the egg yolk mixture. • Whip the remaining cream and fold into the egg mixture. • Divide the mixture between two bowls, placing one-third of the mixture in one, and two-thirds in the other. • Scrape the vanilla pod and mix into the larger mixture. • Gently fold the chocolate into the smaller mixture. • Pour the vanilla mixture into dariole molds or medium sized ramekin molds to about one-third of the way up the mold. Place on a tray and freeze until firm, 20–30 minutes. • Pour the chocolate mixture in on top and freeze overnight. • To turn the semifreddo out, dip each ramekin base into warm water and shake out. Place on a tray and freeze for a few minutes before transferring to serving plates.

3 oz (90 g) milk chocolate, chopped
2⅓ cups (600 ml) heavy (double) cream
2 large eggs, separated
¾ cup (150 g) superfine (caster) sugar
1 vanilla pod split lengthways

Coffee Granita

Place the sugar in a medium bowl. Pour the hot coffee in over the top and stir until the sugar has completely dissolved. Let cool to room temperature. • Pour the mixture into a plastic or stainless steel container about 10 inches (25 cm) square. Place in the freezer and leave for 1 hour. • Use a fork or hand blender to break the granita up into large crystals. • If using an ice cream machine, transfer to the machine at this point and follow the manufacturer's instructions. • To continue by hand, replace the container in the freezer for 30 minutes, then break up again with a fork. Repeat 3 or 4 times, until the crystals are completely frozen. • Scoop into 2–4 glasses or dessert bowls. Top with the whipped cream, if liked.

½ cup (100 g) sugar

1½ cups (375 ml) very hot strong black coffee

½ cup (125 ml) whipped cream (optional)

Fruit Bombe

Line a domed 1½-quart (1.5-liter) pudding mold or metal bowl with plastic wrap (cling film). Mix the fruit (reserving a few slices to decorate), sugar, and lemon juice in a medium bowl, dissolving the sugar as much as possible. • Stir in the coconut ice cream. • Pack the ice cream mixture into the prepared bowl. Freeze for 12 hours. • Soften the strawberry ice cream at room temperature, 10 minutes. Turn the bombe out onto a serving dish. Remove the wrap. Spread with the strawberry ice cream nd decorate with the reserved fruit. Freeze for at least 1 hour before serving.

1 cup (150 g) fresh raspberries
½ cup fresh red currants
(or additional raspberries)
2 apricots, pitted and chopped
1 large peach, peeled, pitted
and chopped
2 kiwifruit, peeled and chopped
½ cup (100 g) sugar
2 tablespoons freshly squeezed lemon
juice
1 lb (500 g) coconut or peach ice
cream, softened
1 lb (500 g) strawberry ice cream,
softened

Zuccotto

Mix the sugar and water in a saucepan over medium heat until the sugar has dissolved and it comes to a boil. Boil for 5 minutes. Remove from the heat. Add the brandy and rum and let cool. • Moisten the edges of a domed 2-quart (2-liter) mold or metal bowl with a little syrup and line with half the cake slices. Brush with the remaining syrup. • Beat the cream until thick. Gently fold the confectioners' sugar, nuts, candied fruit, and 5 oz (150 g) of chocolate into the cream. Spoon the cream into the mold and top with the remaining cake slices. • Refrigerate for 5 hours. • Dip the mold briefly into cold water. Invert onto a serving plate. Sprinkle with the remaining grated chocolate and serve.

- 1 cup (200 g) sugar
- 1 cup (250 ml) water
- 3 tablespoons brandy
- 3 tablespoons rum
- 1 Basic Sponge Cake (see page 46), cut into 1/4-inch (5-mm) thick slices
- 2 cups (500 ml) heavy (double) cream
- 1/3 cup (50 g) confectioners' (icing) sugar
- 1/3 cup (40 g) almonds, finely ground
- 1/3 cup (40 g) hazelnuts, finely ground
- 1/4 cup (40 g) mixed candied fruit, chopped
- 6 oz (180 g) dark chocolate, grated

45

SERVES 6–8

PREPARATION 1 h + 12 h to chill

COOKING 35–45 min

DIFFICULTY level 3

Gelato Cake
with chocolate and candied fruit

Basic Sponge Cake: Preheat the oven to 350°F (180°C/gas 4). • Butter a 9-inch (23-cm) springform pan. Line the pan with parchment paper. • Mix the flour and salt in a medium bowl. • Beat the egg yolks, sugar, and lemon zest in a large bowl with an electric mixer on high speed until pale and very thick. • Beat the egg whites in a large bowl until stiff peaks form. Use a large rubber spatula to fold the dry ingredients into the egg yolk mixture. Carefully fold in the beaten whites. • Working quickly, spoon the batter into the prepared pan. Bake until springy to the touch and the cake shrinks from the pan sides, 35–45 minutes. • Cool the cake in the pan for 5 minutes. Loosen and remove the pan sides. Invert the cake onto a rack. Loosen and remove the pan bottom. Carefully remove the paper. Turn the cake top-side up and let cool completely. • Gelato Cake: Line a 1½-quart (1.5-liter) mold or a stainless steel bowl with plastic wrap (cling film). • Thinly slice the sponge and dip in the rum until moist. Line the prepared mold with the cake slices. • Melt the chocolate with 2 tablespoons of rum and the coffee in a double boiler over barely simmering water. • Set aside to cool. • Beat 2 cups (500 ml) of cream, confectioners' sugar, and vanilla in a large bowl until stiff. • Gently fold half the cream into the melted chocolate. • Fold the candied fruit and almonds into the remaining cream. • Spoon the chocolate mixture into the mold. Spoon the candied fruit cream over the top, smoothing the top. • Cover with aluminum foil and refrigerate for 12 hours, or overnight. • Invert and turn out the mold onto a serving plate. • Beat the remaining cream in a medium bowl until stiff. Spread the cream over the top and dust with the cocoa.

Basic Sponge Cake
1 cup (150 g) all-purpose (plain) flour
¼ teaspoon salt
6 large eggs, separated
1¼ cups (250 g) sugar
½ tablespoon finely grated lemon zest

Gelato Cake
¼ cup (60 ml) rum
3 oz (90 g) dark chocolate, chopped
2 tablespoons instant coffee granules
2½ cups (600 ml) heavy (double) cream
2 tablespoons confectioners' (icing) sugar
1 teaspoon vanilla extract (essence)
⅓ cup (60 g) chopped mixed candied fruit
½ cup (50 g) chopped almonds
⅓ cup (50 g) unsweetened cocoa powder

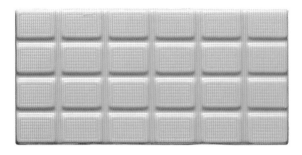

Parfait
with white chocolate

Line a 9 x 5-inch (23 x 18-cm) terrine mold or loaf pan with plastic wrap (cling film). • Melt the white chocolate in a double boiler over barely simmering water. Set aside. • Beat the egg yolks in a large bowl with an electric mixer at high speed until pale and thick. • Mix the superfine sugar and water in a small saucepan over medium heat, stirring often, until the sugar has dissolved. Bring to a boil. • Decrease the heat to low and simmer for 3 minutes. • With the mixer at low speed, gradually beat the syrup into the beaten egg yolks. Beat until the mixture has cooled. Stir in the chocolate. • Use a large rubber spatula to fold in the whipped cream. • Pour the mixture into the prepared mold. • Cover with plastic wrap and freeze overnight. • Cut into slices and serve.

6 oz (180 g) white chocolate, coarsely chopped
5 large egg yolks
1/2 cup (100 g) superfine (caster) sugar
1/4 cup (60 ml) water
1 2/3 cups (400 ml) whipped cream

Gelato Cake
Sicilian style

Place a 1½-quart (1.5-liter) pudding mold in the freezer. • Stir the green food coloring into the softened gelato. Place the chopped candied fruit in a small bowl and pour the rum over the top. Let macerate for 30 minutes. • When the pudding mold is very cold, line it with the pistachio gelato. Use a dessert spoon dipped into ice water to smooth the gelato. • Beat the egg white and confectioners' sugar with an electric mixer on high speed until stiff. Beat the cream in a separate bowl until thick then fold into the egg white mixture. Stir the candied fruit and rum into the mixture. • Fill the center of the cake with the cream mixture and freeze for at least 3 hours. • To serve, run the mold quickly under cold running water, taking care that the water doesn't get on the cake. Place a serving plate over the mold and tip the cake out onto it.

1 quantity Pistachio Gelato (see page 56), softened
1 teaspoon green food coloring
1 cup (100 g) mixed candied fruit, chopped
¼ cup (60 ml) white rum
1 large egg white
5 tablespoons confectioners' (icing) sugar
1 cup (250 ml) heavy (double) cream

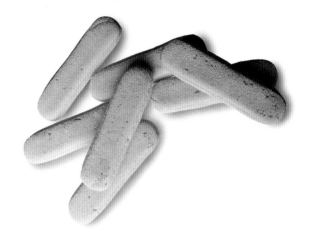

Frozen Tiramisù

Line the base and sides of a 9 x 5-inch (23 x 12-cm) loaf pan with aluminum foil. • Beat the egg yolks and sugar with an electric mixer on high speed until pale and creamy. • Beat in the mascarpone. • Beat the egg whites and salt with an electric mixer on high speed until stiff peaks form. • Beat the cream until thickened. • Fold the egg whites and cream into the mascarpone mixture. • Mix the coffee and brandy, if using, in a bowl. • Place a layer of ladyfingers in the loaf pan. Brush with the coffee mixture and cover with a layer of the mascarpone mixture. Repeat this layering process until all the ingredients are in the pan. • Cover the pan with foil and freeze for at least 4 hours. • To serve, run a long sharp knife down the sides of the pan and turn out onto a serving plate. Let rest for 5 minutes before serving.

4 large eggs, separated
$^1/_2$ cup (100 g) sugar
2 cups (500 g) mascarpone cheese
$^1/_8$ teaspoon salt
$^1/_2$ cup (125 ml) heavy (double) cream
4 oz (125 g) ladyfingers
    (sponge fingers)
$^1/_2$ cup (125 ml) strong black coffee
1 tablespoon brandy (optional)

Semifeddo

with chocolate and coconut

Dampen a sheet of parchment paper with the orange flower water. Use the paper to line a 9 x 5-inch (23 x 12-cm) loaf pan. • Process the ricotta, sugar, coconut, and vanilla in a food processor until well smooth. • Stir in the chocolate. • Beat the cream in a large bowl with an electric mixer on high speed until stiff, then carefully fold it into the ricotta mixture. • Spoon the mixture into the prepared loaf pan. • Freeze for 4 hours. • Turn the semifreddo out onto a serving platter. • Decorate with the fruit and serve in thick slices.

1 teaspoon orange flower water
$1\frac{1}{4}$ cups (300 g) ricotta, drained
$\frac{3}{4}$ cup (150 g) sugar
$\frac{3}{4}$ cup (90 g) unsweetened shredded (desiccated) coconut
$\frac{1}{2}$ teaspoon vanilla extract (essence)
4 oz (125 g) dark chocolate, chopped
2 cups (500 ml) heavy (double) cream
2 kiwifruit, sliced
2 star anise
1 ripe mango, cut in segments
1 ripe papaya (pawpaw), cut in segments

Gelato Cake
Neapolitan style

Pistachio Gelato: Preheat the oven to 350°F (180°C/gas 4). Arrange the pistachios and almonds on a baking sheet and toast until lightly browned, 5–10 minutes. Transfer to a food processor and chop with 1/4 cup (50 g) of sugar and the water to make a smooth paste. • Place the milk, cream, lemon zest, and pistachio paste in a heavy-based saucepan over medium heat and bring to a boil. Remove from the heat and discard the lemon zest. • Beat the egg yolks, vanilla, and remaining sugar in a large bowl with an electric mixer on high speed until pale and creamy. • Pour the hot milk and pistachio mixture into the egg yolk mixture, beating constantly with a wooden spoon. Return to the saucepan and simmer over very low heat, stirring constantly, until the mixture just coats the back of the spoon. Do not let the mixture boil. • Remove from the heat. Let cool, stirring often. Chill in the refrigerator for 30 minutes. • Stir in the green food coloring, if using. Transfer the mixture to an ice cream machine and freeze following the manufacturer's instructions. • Prepare the Chocolate Gelato. • Line a 9-inch (23-cm) springform pan with parchment paper. • Soak the cherries in the kirsch for 1 hour. • Cut the sponge cake in half horizontally. Place one layer of sponge cake in the prepared pan. Freeze for 30 minutes. (The rest can be frozen for future use). • Drain the cherries, reserving the kirsch. Drizzle the kirsch over the cake. Spread with half the pistachio gelato (The rest can be frozen for future use). • Arrange the cherries on top of the gelato and spread with the chocolate gelato. • Freeze for 4 hours. • Unloosen and remove the pan sides. Place the cake on a serving plate. Dust with the confectioners' sugar and top with the cherries.

Pistachio Gelato
3/4 cup (120 g) blanched pistachios
Generous 1/4 cup (50 g) blanched almonds
1 cup (200 g) granulated sugar
2 tablespoons water
2 cups (500 ml) milk
2 cups (500 ml) heavy (double) cream
Zest of 1/2 a lemon, removed using a sharp knife
7 large egg yolks
1 teaspoon vanilla extract (essence)
Few drops of green food coloring, optional

1 Basic Sponge Cake (see page 46)

1/2 cup (70 g) candied cherries, chopped
1 cup (250 ml) kirsch
2 cups (500 g) Chocolate Gelato (see page 63), softened
1/4 cup (30 g) confectioners' (icing) sugar, to dust
Candied cherries, to decorate

SERVES 4–6

PREPARATION 15 min + 30 min to chill
and time to churn

COOKING 15 min

DIFFICULTY level 1

Chocolate Sorbet

Place the chocolate in a double boiler over barely simmering water. Stir occasionally until melted. Remove from the heat and let cool slightly. • Place the sugar and water in a saucepan over medium heat and stir until the sugar has dissolved. • Stir in the chocolate. Remove from the heat. Let cool to room temperature. Chill in the refrigerator for 30 minutes. • Place the mixture in an ice cream machine and churn according to the manufacturer's instructions. • If you don't have an ice cream machine, place the chocolate syrup in a metal bowl and freeze. When the mixture has just begun to set, whisk it with an electric beater or by hand, until creamy. Repeat at least 3 or 4 more times, or until the sorbet is thick and smooth.

8 oz (250 g) dark chocolate, finely chopped

2 cups (500 ml) water

1 cup (200 g) sugar

Prosecco Sorbet
in sugar snap baskets

Preheat the oven to 375° F (190°C/gas 5). • Sugar Snap Baskets: Beat the sugar, flour, butter, and egg whites in a bowl with an electric mixer on medium speed to make a smooth batter. • Oil a large nonstick baking sheet. Place 8–10 spoonfuls of the mixture on the prepared baking sheet, making sure that they are well spaced because they will spread during baking. • Bake for 7–10 minutes, until well spread and lightly browned. Remove from the oven and let cool slightly. • Brush the outsides of 8–10 ramekins or small molds with a little oil. Place the sugar snaps over the ramekins, pressing them lightly so that they fit the molds. Let cool. Carefully slip the cooled, crisp baskets off the molds. • Prosecco Sorbet: Combine the sugar and water in a large saucepan over medium heat and bring to a boil. Simmer until the sugar has completely dissolved, 2–3 minutes. Remove from the heat and let cool completely. • Beat the egg white and confectioners' sugar in a double boiler over barely simmering water until thick and glossy, 5–10 minutes. Remove from the heat. • Carefully stir the prosecco and meringue mixture into the sugar syrup. Transfer to an ice-cream maker and churn according to the manufacturer's instructions. • Spoon the sorbet into the sugar snap baskets. Garnish with slices of fresh fruit and serve at once.

Sugar Snap Baskets
Generous 1/3 cup (75 g) sugar
1/3 cup (75 g) all-purpose (plain) flour
1/4 cup (60 g) salted butter, melted
2 large egg whites

Prosecco Sorbet
1 3/4 cups (350 g) sugar
1 1/2 cups (375 ml) water
1 large egg white
1/2 cup (75 g) confectioners' (icing) sugar
2 cups (500 ml) Italian Prosecco or dry Champagne
Fresh fruit, sliced, to serve

Gelato Torte

Meringue: Preheat the oven to 200°F (110°C/gas ½). • Mix both types of sugar in a bowl. • Beat the egg whites in a large bowl with an electric mixer on high speed until stiff. Add the sugar mixture gradually, beating constantly, until thick and glossy. • Line two baking sheets with parchment paper. Use a pencil and the base of a 9-inch (23-cm) springform pan to draw three circles onto the paper. • Spoon the meringue onto the disks. • Bake until dry and crisp, about 90 minutes. Remove from the oven and let cool. • Nougat Gelato: Place the milk, cream, and sugar in a heavy-based saucepan over medium heat and stir until the sugar has dissolved. Remove from the heat and let cool. Add the cognac. • Transfer to an ice cream machine and churn following the manufacturer's instructions. When the gelato is almost frozen add the nougat. • Place the gelato in the freezer. • Chocolate Gelato: Place the milk and vanilla pod in a large saucepan over medium heat and bring to a boil. • Beat the egg yolks and sugar in a bowl with mixer on high speed until pale and creamy. Gradually add the milk mixture, beating with a wooden spoon. Discard the vanilla pod. Return the mixture to the saucepan. Simmer over low heat, stirring constantly, until it just coats the back of the spoon. Do not let it boil. • Remove from the heat and stir in the chocolate. Let cool. • Transfer to an ice cream machine and churn following the manufacturer's instructions. • Line a 10-inch (25-cm) springform pan with parchment paper. • Let both types of gelato stand at room temperature for 10 minutes to soften. • Place one of the meringue disks in the pan. Spread with the nougat gelato. Add another meringue disk. Spread with the chocolate gelato. Top with the remaining meringue disk. Freeze for 2 hours. • Beat the cream in a large bowl until thick. • Unmold the torte and decorate with the cream. Sprinkle with chocolate and serve.

Meringue
⅓ cup (50 g) confectioners' (icing) sugar
¼ cup (50 g) superfine (caster) sugar
2 large egg whites

Nougat Gelato
1 cup (250 ml) milk
1 cup (250 ml) heavy (double) cream
¾ cup (150 g) sugar
1 tablespoon cognac
2 oz (60 g) firm nougat, finely chopped

Chocolate Gelato
2 cups (500 ml) milk
1 vanilla pod, sliced open lengthwise
4 large egg yolks
¾ cup (150 g) sugar
4 oz (125 g) dark) chocolate, chopped

2 cups (500 ml) heavy (double) cream
Dark chocolate, grated, to decorate

Index

Copyright © 2009 by McRae Books Srl

This English edition first published in 2009

All rights reserved. No part of this book may be reproduced in any form without the prior written permission of the publisher and copyright owner.

Gelato

was created and produced by McRae Books Srl

Via del Salviatino 1 – 50016 Fiesole, (Florence) Italy

info@mcraebooks.com

Publishers: Anne McRae and Marco Nardi

Project Director: Anne McRae

Design: Sara Mathews

Text: McRae Books archive

Editing: Carla Bardi

Photography: Studio Lanza (Lorenzo Borri, Cristina Canepari, Ke-ho Casati, Mauro Corsi, Gil Gallo, Leonardo Pasquinelli, Gianni Petronio, Stefano Pratesi, Sandra Preussinger)

Home Economist: Benedetto Rillo

Artbuying: McRae Books

Layouts: Aurora Granata, Filippo Delle Monache, Davide Gasparri

Repro: Fotolito Raf, Florence

ISBN 978-88-6098-084-7

Printed and bound in China